I0407916

Mandala
Amazing Coloring Books

Copyright: Published in the United States by Alana Duff
Published January 2017
ISBN-13: 978-1542679992
ISBN-10: 1542679990

Thank you

www.ingramcontent.com/pod-product-compliance
Lightning Source LLC
Chambersburg PA
CBHW081554280526
45788CB00011B/3471